Praise for Melina Lovera's *Rebirth*

"Melina Lovera's poetry collection, *Rebirth*, is a full-length novel that honors the power of love, vulnerability, and renewal. Her sophomore collection is simply a continuation of Awakening. This assortment of poems shows the reader that one can be soft and powerful at the same time. Honoring how one can truly find rebirth by focusing on self-love. Melina is one of the four Ambassadors in my program, and I'm truly fascinated by the growth that she has found in herself and writing. She has been a great team player along with others, and her positive energy is infectious! I can't wait for you all to read her collection!"

— Celeste Alyssa Gomez,
Author & Founder of La Poeta Publications

"*Rebirth*, Melina Lovera's second collection of poems and songs, is a stunning exploration of heartbreak, healing, and transformation. Through lyrics that blend elements of both poetry and songwriting, she depicts a portrait of womanhood that is as confessional as it is universal - meditating on past mistakes, sitting in grief, realizing the true worth and value of your body, mind, and spirit. As Lovera moves into this next hopeful phase of her life, so do we follow, waiting with bated breath."

— Sofía Aguilar,
author of *amor.* and STREAMING SERVICE: *the series finale*

"*Rebirth* is a powerful collection of poems. From the pain of lost love to the courage of starting over, Melina leads us through an unapologetic journey of healing, growth, and resilience. Written in English, with select poems in Spanish, she shows that starting again is not just natural, it is essential, especially for women reclaiming our power. Rebirth is an act of strength, a declaration of self-worth, and the essence of true human evolution."

— Virginia Bulacio,
author of *Luna Inmigrante*

"*Rebirth* is the irreplacable product of that thing all writers and artists aspire to obtain: true, raw, authentic experience. Melina undresses the mysteries of love, womanhood, and healing in a masterful collection of poetry that is not so soon to be forgotten or overlooked."

— Joan Abigail Mabansag,
Editor & Graphic Design Lead, La Poeta Publications

"Have you ever had to grieve a version of yourself that never got to happen? In this collection by Melina Lovera, the reader is guided through the claustrophobic grief of letting go; not just of a person, but of a carefully imagined future. These poems offer a steady-handed grace, capturing the jagged discomfort of unlearning the sacrifice of self and the quiet, subterranean growth required to survive emotional chaos. It is a raw, bilingual anthem for anyone who has ever had to break their own heart to save their own soul."

— Jean-Pierre Rueda
Award-winning author of
Amor Entre Aguaceros/Love Between Downpours,
Juan Felipe Herrera Award for Best Poetry Book Bilingual ILBA 2025\

"*Rebirth* offers you company inside what is kept quiet: what it costs to love someone who doesn't love you back, about the specific way you disappear, piece by piece, trying to become what they need. About the morning you wake up and don't recognize the person you've become, but with the particularity of Lovera's witness, these words become a bridge as a way across. Melina Lovera's debut full-length collection moves through heartbreak the way healing actually happens, with fracture logic only poetry can hold. Poems threaded in the collection anchor devastation in English—on the specific months and dates your mind can't erase, on bathroom floors, at five in the morning, on street corners where everything ended—then reach for Spanish when English can't hold the possibility of what comes next. When Lovera pens the lines 'Ámame libre,' it's the refusal to earn your own affection, to yearn for what is unconditional. 'Vida tranquila' rejects chaos and toxic intensity for a life anew. 'Sale el sol' carries spiritual weight, ancestral understandings that English platitudes can't touch. By 'Renacer,' you understand why some transformations can only be named in the language you were born into. The confessional language in *Rebirth* doesn't flinch. Organized into three sections—Soil, Roots, Bloom—these poems hold contradictions at once, in both protection and vulnerability, and rage and tenderness. This collection is for anyone learning how the bliss to choose themselves, over and over, becomes the only choice worth cultivating the ground beneath you."

— Shandela Contreras,
award-winning spoken-word poet & author of
Every Beautiful Pen Bleeds Through

"In *Rebirth*, Melina Lovera depicts—with honesty and vulnerability—the aftermath of a failing and abusive relationship. Continuing from Awakening, this collection moves forward, navigating the emotional terrain of healing while confronting its realities. As she writes, 'The bravest thing I ever did was leave / It took everything in me,' grounding the work in both courage and cost.

From first dates to wrestling with nostalgia, longing, and lingering trauma, Lovera captures the complexity of starting over: "'Fear starts creeping in. What if we don't last / I can't survive reliving my past.' Even in moments of quiet, healing resists simplicity—"Healing did not arrive as relief." Instead, it unfolds slowly, unevenly, through reflection and reckoning.

At times, the work is filled with lament for a past that still lingers—'I still hear the echoes of your voice screaming... / My phone is bouncing off the dresser door'—revealing the weight of what was endured, even when minimized: 'And no, he never hit me, so it wasn't abuse.' Through these lines, Lovera challenges the narratives we tell ourselves to survive.

Rebirth traces the painful process of piecing oneself back together—'Growth was not beautiful at first. It was uncomfortable'—as it moves through cycles of learning and unlearning, acknowledging and forgiving. Beginning again is both liberating and intimidating, a space where identity must be rebuilt: 'everything inside was rearranging. My identity was no longer defined by who loved me.'

Ultimately, Lovera arrives at a hard-earned clarity. Even in reflecting on the person who caused her pain, she finds space to hold the lessons: 'You taught me lessons, because of you, I'm careful now when I stumble.' In this way, Rebirth becomes not just a story of survival, but a testament to transformation—of choosing oneself, again and again.

— Alexis Jaimes,
author of *Corazón Coalesced* and *The Seeds We Sow.*

REBIRTH

melina lovera

Translations by Pablo Contreras Sánchez

Photography by Curtis Robideau

Cover Design & Interior Formatting
by Joan Abigail Mabansag

Printed in the United States of America

First Printing, 2026
ISBN 979-8-9869099-5-0
La Poeta Publications
www.LaPoetaPublications.com

To the women who carry storms within them
and still choose to bloom.

To the survivors of trauma,
the ones learning to rebuild themselves piece by piece.

May these words remind you
that even after the darkest nights,
Rebirth is always possible.

Table of Contents

Part III – Bloom

Introduction

Hi, my name is Melina Lovera. I was born in South America, Uruguay. I was raised in Huntington Beach, CA. I have a women's empowerment brand and blog. I am thrilled to share with you my first full collection of poetry, *Rebirth*, a series of songs and poems I wrote in my twenties. Turning every disappointment into art, and learning that life is a journey, we sometimes have to walk the road less traveled to gain mental clarity, maturity, and spiritually evolve as humans. From getting married young, being divorced, and starting over while undergoing a self-discovery journey, to creating Shop Lovera.

This book was written for young women who are brave enough to make mistakes, to fall deeply, and to rise anyway. It is for those who have loved with open hearts, trusted too easily, stayed too long, and eventually learned that growth often comes disguised as loss. I hope these pages remind readers that failure is not a flaw but a teacher, and that dreams are not meant to be abandoned simply because the road toward them is difficult.

Poetry has always been my safe haven, the place I run to when reality feels overwhelming. It has been my way of making sense of pain, of turning heartbreak into language, and of finding beauty in moments that once felt unbearable. Writing has allowed me to escape, to heal, and ultimately to awaken the strongest version of myself. Through this book, I invite others to do the same to pause, reflect, and reconnect with who they truly are beneath the expectations and noise of the world.

Rebirth is the continuation of my first book, *Awakening*, written now from the perspective of my thirties as I look back on my twenties with honesty and compassion. It explores themes of inner healing, unresolved trauma, healthy boundaries, and the quiet courage it takes to love oneself again. This book is not about erasing the past, but about understanding it, honoring it, and learning how to begin again with intention and self-respect.

The structure of *Rebirth* mirrors the natural process of growth. The first section, **Soil**, represents the breaking—the dirt, the betrayal, and the emotional unraveling that comes from loving deeply and losing oneself in what once felt safe. It speaks to walking away from comfort, from toxic love, and from versions of life that no longer align with who we are becoming. This is the stage where everything falls apart, so something truer can take its place.

The second section, **Roots**, is where healing begins in the unseen. It captures the slow and often uncomfortable process of transformation: letting go of old behaviors, unlearning survival patterns, and rediscovering identity in the aftermath of loss. Set in my mid-twenties, this section reflects the quiet work of rebuilding from within, where growth happens before it is visible.

The final section, **Bloom**, is about emergence. It is about becoming someone new while carrying the wisdom of past mistakes. Here, self-love is no longer conditional, and growth feels earned rather than forced. This is where I learn to love myself again, not by returning to who I was, but by embracing who I have become.

Rebirth is a reminder that starting over is not a weakness, but an act of self-trust. It is proof that even after breaking, we are still capable of growth, beauty, and becoming.

You can listen to this curated playlist on *Spotify* -
Rebirth by Lovera

***Unica** x Greeicy (eskia)
***Querida Yo** Alexa Sotelo'
*** Cabron yo Puedo** Mario Bautista
*** Victoria's Secret** Jax
***El Amor de Tu Vida** Dave Bolano
*** Me Levante** Dave Bolano
***I'm still standing** Elton John
***Independent with you** Kylie Morgan
*** Wish you well** Wrabel
***Whiskey Sour** Kane Brown
***29** Carly Pearce
***What He Didn't Do** Carly Pearce
***Confia** Sech Daddy Yankee
***Amor del Bueno** Joey Montana
***Ran into you Mitch Rossell**
***I Don't Know about You** Chris Lane
***La Estrategia** Cali Y El Dandee
***El Chico del Apt 512** Selena
***Brindo** Mario Bautista
***La Independiente** Pitizion
***Llegaste a mi Vida** Yahir
***Cuss a Little** Kylie Morgan
***Mami** Becky G Karol G
***El Barco** Karol G
***Vacation** Dirty Heads
***One of Them Girls** Lee Brice
***Look What God Gave Her** Thomas Rhett
***Better Than you're use to** Tyler Rich
***WYD now** Sadie Jean
***Se Pone mas Bonita** Sierna Miler

*Melancolicos Anónimos Sebastian Yatra

*Tacones Rojos Sebastian Yatra

*See You Later (ten years) Jenna Raine

*Written in the Sand Old Dominion

*From the Ground Up Dan & Shay

*Prayed for You Matt Stell

* La Curiosidad Jay Wheeler

*Llegaste Tu CNCO

*Quizas Tony Dize

*Tequila Dan & Shay

*No Sigue Modas Juan Magan

*Pase Lo Que Pase Joey Montana

*Picky Joey Montana

*Buy Dirt Jordan Davis, Luke Bryan

*DPM Kany Garcia

*Not Suppose to know Each other Taylor Edwards

*Que Haríamos los Viernes Karen Mendez

*No es No Pitizion

*Gracias a Ti Pitizion

*Crisis Mentales Pitizion

*Ella Pitizion

*Own Roses Nikita Karmen

*Ela E Hit Greeicy

*Los Consejos Greeicy

*Color Esperanza Diego Torres

*Caraluna Basilcos

*Leave her Wild Tyler Rich

*Saturno Pablo Alborán

*No Es Cierto Dana Paola

*Entra en Mi Vida Sin Banderas

*Pero te Conoci Reik

*Rosas La Oreja de Van Gogh

*Titanic Kany Garcia

*Antología Shakira

SOIL

Where breaking, survival, and self-awareness begin.

There was a time in my life when I confused comfort with love.

I stayed in places that hurt me because they were familiar. I held on to people who could not hold me back in the same way, and I called it patience. I called it loyalty. I called it hope. The truth is, I was afraid of what would happen if I let go. I thought losing someone meant losing the version of myself I had built around them.

I didn't notice how slowly I was disappearing. It didn't happen all at once. It happened in small silences, in swallowed feelings, in nights I cried quietly so no one would think I was asking for too much. I learned how to shrink my needs so love would stay. I learned how to apologize for my emotions. I learned how to carry the weight of two people while convincing myself I was strong for doing it.

When things finally broke, I called it a failure. I thought I had ruined something good. I replayed memories searching for the exact moment everything changed, as if I could fix the past by understanding it. But the breaking wasn't the tragedy. The breaking was the truth surfacing. It was the moment I could no longer pretend that love and pain were the same thing.

Leaving felt like tearing apart a life I had memorized. I had to walk away from what I knew, from who I thought I was supposed to be, and from the belief that staying longer would eventually make me loved the way I needed. I didn't feel brave. I felt lost. I felt empty. I felt like I had nowhere to place all the love I still carried.

This section lives in that space — the dirt, the confusion, the grief of letting go not only of a person, but of a future I had already imagined. It is the part of my life where everything fell apart.

I did not know then that nothing real was ending.

Something real was beginning.

September 24 2019

The fireworks were lighting up the sky
Post Malone was singing I'm too good at goodbyes
Lately, all we do is fight
And I just about had enough of pouring from an empty cup
I asked for one simple favor that you couldn't do
I said don't get too drunk
Whatever you do, I'm begging you

But it was 9 am, and there was Jack in your cup
That was my last straw
And we were screaming at each other
And you're telling me I'm gonna leave you
It's either you or my family, but I have to choose

I said I do,
I signed my life away at 22
But it was too good to be true
I said I'm over this shit
I needed a companion and friend, a lover til death do us part
But you will always be the boy who broke my heart

I said I'm done with tears in my eyes
Walking down Fremont Street
You couldn't be the man I wanted you to be
And the worst part is, I loved you more than me

I texted our mutual friend.
Please let me know when he gets to the hotel
Don't leave him alone, and please hide his keys
I ran to the restroom and threw up that night

Anxiety-driven shaking inside
My sister and friends are sleeping through the entire drive
That 5 am call...I'll leave the details between him and I
My mother is crying in the background
He calls her a bitch, and I am listening to how this can't be fixed

The difficult conversation happened next.
My dad said you know, here you will always have a home
The choice is yours
But if I were you, I would have walked away a long time ago

Aftermath

The first week was the worst.
I had to force myself to eat rice that tasted like chalk
Be professional at work
She is so skinny and so depressed
The office chatter, people love to talk

My mama let me cry for three days straight
And on the fourth day, she said you're getting back up
She used to make me tea to calm my anxiety
I used to smoke the night away like it was a remedy

Each September, I decorated my body with new ink
as a sign that I was healing.
I dyed my hair every shade of the rainbow
And I confess I slept in strangers' beds
Cuz someone gave me bad advice
And I thought I was damaged inside

It's been six years now.
And I never went back to Life Is Beautiful festival
The hardest thing I've ever did was leave
He signed the papers eventually

I stopped feeling guilty.
And the healing came.

In our last conversation, we admitted we were young
But too much has happened that can't be undone
He wanted a second chance
Said maybe in another life we get it right
Maybe in another life it's you and I

What he didn't do played on the radio
As I passed by his house for the last time
I felt the weight lift off my shoulders
And I started to become stronger

The Hardest Thing I Ever Did

The bravest thing I ever did was leave
It took everything in me
But I hung on, thinking that with time,
you'll be the man I fell in love with at the start.
But you kept being the man who kept breaking my heart.

nineteen and twenty-three, I want different things
Maybe life hit me harder and made me grow up faster
I still hear the echoes of your voice screaming
Still see the shattered glass cups as I am leaving
My phone is bouncing off the dresser door

I was begging you to stop with tears in my eyes
Telling myself little white lies
It's the last time
Won't happen again
 He said he will work on his temper and quit drinking whiskey
I was contemplating leaving, but feeling guilty

We won't have this conversation again.
And no, he never hit me, so it wasn't abuse
Drinking was just the cover-up or the excuse
Silently losing myself
No, I'm fine, it was just a bad day
I don't need help
It's the ups and downs addicted to the roller coaster merry-go-round

But September 24th
I was sitting crying, locked in a bathroom floor
Telling myself the real truth
If I stay, I'll be dead by June

I could cut little cuts with the pieces of the glass
I hated those thoughts
I loved him more than I loved myself
I had to pick up the pieces of me from the shelf

The smiles were the cover-up.
Picture-perfect life, happy wife

The hardest thing I've ever did was leave
But time did what it had to do
And slowly the love died too

I dyed my hair every color of the rainbow
Decorated my body with new ink each September
Swallowed the pain and promised never to love again

Let Me Be Naive

Let me go back to nineteen.
Let me be naive, let me be gullible, and believe
Subscribed to Cosmopolitan and Seventeen magazines
Watch too many rom coms, read all the teen fiction books on aisle four

Let me be naive, so when you say you'll stay with me, let me be naive
You're different from the rest, and I'm not quite yet a mess
Cuz at twenty-five there's enough damage to go around

Grab my keys, and I'm hitting downtown
It's a Friday night, and I wanna feel alive
Let me be naive, and you tread softly
Whisper in my ear all the things I wanna hear
Let me be naive as you undress me with your eyes
As you seduce me with your lies

Let me be naive
Fuck me like tomorrow you won't say goodbye
You think I'm funny, I'm cute, and super cool
You're falling, and you're not leaving. You can read me
But you don't know
I'm an actress, and I've got this act down to perfection
Baby, you're just playing this game of seduction
We are each other's addiction
This electricity is rushing through my body like ecstasy
let's pretend we're a couple of high school kids, the summer before it all ends

Let's be naive
Let's be naive
Let me be naive

Déjame ser ingenua

Déjame volver a los diecinueve
Déjame ser ingenua, déjame ser crédula, déjame creer
Suscrita a Cosmopolitan y a la revista Seventeen,
ver demasiadas comedias románticas,
 leer todos los libros de ficción adolescente del pasillo cuatro

Déjame ser ingenua,
para que cuando digas que te quedarás conmigo, yo te crea
Eres distinto a los demás, y yo todavía no soy un desastre,
porque a los veinticinco ya hay suficiente daño para repartir.

Agarro mis llaves y me voy al centro
Es viernes por la noche y quiero sentirme viva
Déjame ser ingenua, y camina con cuidado
Susúrrame al oído todo lo que quiero oír
Déjame ser ingenua mientras me desnudas con la mirada,
mientras me seduces con tus mentiras

Déjame ser ingenua
Cógeme como si mañana no fueras a decir adiós
Crees que soy graciosa, linda y súper cool
Te estás enamorando y no te vas a ir. Puedes leerme,
pero no sabes que soy actriz,
y tengo este papel dominado a la perfección
Nene, tú solo estás jugando este juego de seducción
Somos la adicción del otro
Esta electricidad corre por mi cuerpo como éxtasis
finjamos que somos un par de estudiantes de prepa,
el verano antes de que todo termine

Seamos ingenuos
Seamos ingenuos
Déjame ser ingenua.

Today

Today I looked again at that album,
the one I tried so hard to erase,
the one that now is set to private
so no one comes invading my space.

The one that brings back that young girl
who slowly turned into a woman
within the four walls of your bedroom
where we made love, slow and human.

Damn these memories and photographs,
they pull me to a cruel fantasy.
I thought that you were perfect once,
I gave my life so carelessly.

What we had was pure illusion,
a fragile, shining fantasy.
Lies and quiet hypocrisy,
dreams of a reckless girl in love,
who loved you far beyond all reason
until she woke and had enough
until the day goodbye arrived.

Today it's been a year exactly
since that fragile dream was gone.
How sad that everything would end
with just my signature alone.

I hope that life is kind to you,
that everything goes well somehow.
Today I raise a glass to that illusion
that once brought you and me together,
that made us tremble, made us fly,
that made us feel that we knew love forever.

Nineteen years old, she left her home,
a foolish girl, in love and blind.
She trusted fully in the fantasy,
never seeing the lie behind.
You were the greatest mistake
I ever carried in my life.

Hoy

Hoy he vuelto a ver ese álbum
El que he intentado de borrar
Ese que hoy está en privado
Pa que nadie venga a molestar

El que me recuerda a esa niña
Que en mujer se convirtió
En las cuatro paredes de tu habitación
Dónde lentamente hacíamos el amor

Malditos recuerdos y fotografías
Me llevan a mi cruel fantasía
Te creía perfecto
Te entregué mi vida
Lo nuestro fue pura fantasía

Mentiras y hipocresía
Sueños de una loca niña
Que te amo sin medida
Hasta que se despertó
Y llegó la despedida

Hoy hace un año que el sueño acabó
Qué triste que todo termine con mi firma
en un papel
Espero que a ti te vaya muy bien
Hoy brindo por la fantasía que nos unió
Qué nos hizo vibrar que no hizo volar
Qué nos hizo sentir que sabíamos amar

19 años y se fue de casa
Chica tonta loca enamorada
Se creyó su fantasía
No vio la realidad de la mentira
Fuiste el gran error de mi vida

No Trust in Us

Every time I try to let you in and trust you.
You let me down. You say you won't do it again,
and I get my hopes up, then I watch them fall each time...
And I know you're a master at your craft.

You don't have to lie cuz I can read it in your eyes
You don't have to pretend anymore
I see you're always going to be a revolving door

And here I thought I could finally trust in love
Here I thought you could be the one
But here I am left pretending I don't care
Here I am, left hugging the pillow tight
Pretending you're not there

Here, I thought I could trust
But you're always falling into the same traps
I think your love sounds more like lust
I know I could start over and move on
I've done it before, so it shouldn't take long
But I got used to having you around

Pretending you love me even if your actions prove you don't
I know you're not perfect, and neither am I
But if I can't trust you, this should end with goodbye

It's been three years, baby.
Three years of he will change, maybe
Three years of us it won't happen again
But my patience and my trust are at their wits' end
There's no trust in us

Magnetic Pull

I feel it too, that magnetic pull
Like, no matter what or with who
You live rent-free on my mind
I guess I pushed my feelings aside
Thinking you would never be mine

But tonight the music is loud.
Playing in my head every word you ever said
Like maybe we were just young
And didn't want to try, so we gave up before we started
But we still ended broken-hearted

And throughout the years, we catch up
 and have glimpses of what could have been

You never said you loved me.
So how was I supposed to know
I was more than just a few nights
While you're home alone

You never said a word.
So I left thinking I wasn't yours
I got tired of breaking my own heart
And you treated me like the rest
Maybe you were a lesson I thought I finally passed my test

But I feel it too, the magnetic pull
If the red string theory is true
I think mine is with you

Moon

Moon, I know it's late
for promises and dreams,
Because I feel time is slipping through my fingers.
Could it be the year is almost over,
and I'm living off memories?

Moon, I regret wanting to grow up,
to be someone important...
The routine between home and the office...
I walk around so confused and tired.

Moon, my soul is all in disarray.
Moon, I'm asking you for advice:
How do I keep my calm?

Moon, I want to turn back time,
to freeze every moment and hit replay.
I want to be that little girl again
dancing down the street,
living inside her imaginary world.

Luna

Luna, sé que es tarde
para las promesas y los sueños,
Porque siento que el tiempo se me escapa entre los dedos.
¿Será que casi se acaba el año
¿Y yo vivo de recuerdos?

Luna, me arrepiento de querer ser grande,
alguien importante...
La rutina entre la casa y la oficina...
Ando toda confundida y cansada.

Luna, tengo el alma desordenada.
Luna, te pido un consejo:
¿Cómo hago para mantener la calma?

Luna, quiero volver el tiempo atrás,
Congelar cada momento y darle *replay*.
Quiero volver a ser esa niña que va por la calle bailando,
Viviendo en su mundo imaginario.

Worst Regret

I'm hard to forget
I'm your worst regret
If you walk away
You'll be haunted by my silhouette
We were damaged and young then
But you're still hooked on my lips like nicotine
It's what you said
As you were holding my hips

Steady, you will always be my baby
Can't write you off as a memory
Cuz you were my poison and my remedy
Maybe it's just another ego death
But we're both stuck in this journey
Why does it feel like you never left

You will find me in everyone you meet
Don't be a coward this time
I can understand if you have other plans
But if you love me, you would try

So go and change the world.
Try to make it better.
I can love you and let you go
If that's the price, I'll sacrifice
If we're not meant to be together

But we both know
This is love
We're both scared to fall
Cuz we risked it all once before
We both hate not being in control

I admit it. I was wrong
Couldn't see past my illusions
You were there all along
I just took the blindfold

I'm so sorry
I'm your worst regret you can't forget
I'm the love of your life, even though you lied

Borrowed

I wish things were different.
But damn, the universe and god really had a lesson for me in store
I realized 7 years too late, I was in love with you from the very first day
Maybe a part of me always knew
That's why we were a moth to a flame

You ignited something in me, but then you would leave,
and your absence would consume me.
You lingered on my lips, and I felt you on my skin
Even if I pushed my thoughts away
I always found a way to see you

knowing you were borrowed and wouldn't stay
I used to joke around. You were my full moon guy
The one who would call me with no doubt
Ask me to come over and watch a movie, we never got to see the end

I told you my life story on our first date.
You did the same, we laughed and high-fived each other
on our disastrous first marriages.
I asked you a few years later
If you would ever get married again
We were at a park playing with your dog
You said yes so cheerfully without a doubt

You told me she would be your friend first, and you would take things slow
Then you asked me my thoughts, and I was quick to say no, never again
Then you smiled and said with the right person
You will change your mind

We were on borrowed time.
You never belong to me, although for a glimpse
In the contingent of time and space
You were mine
We made a pact that two divorced people could never work
Something about the statistics being too high
So we never really tried

We could have been epic.
But healing takes time.
When you were single, I was not
And when I was you were not

But every holiday, every summer vacation
We would borrow time
I never told you how I felt
You never said a word
But in the silence, it was understood
We were borrowed

Red String

Red string ties me up in knots
It unravels, I let go, and then it pulls me back again
And the cycle continues on and on
But I only see you as a friend
I lied, I lied, it was easier to run and hide
I lied to your face to avoid all the pain
Red string has never been stronger
I see you as more than a friend, but my lover
Oh, oh, oh, here we go again
We almost said it to eachother
But it was easier to find another
Red string, what are you doing, pulling on my core
Making me open wounds I closed before
Just so I can face my mirror
And speak from my soul
I guess this is love

Parece que el amor

Así como empieza, acaba
Y el tuyo se me escapó de madrugada

No soy nadie para detenerte
Me imaginé una vida contigo
Pero no fue nuestra suerte

Parece que otra vez las cartas no están de mi parte
Parece que sola debo quedarme
Parece que nunca pudiste amarme
Como yo queria
Porque tú tienes dudas mientras yo te di mi vida
Parece que los tiempos no son perfectos
Las circunstancias nos separan
Y yo ya conozco el final

Parece que el amor es raro
Lo tengo malacostumbrado
Parece que esta vez se quiere quedar
Mi terco corazón no sabe de razón

Sometimes I wonder

Sometimes I wonder will you still love me when my beauty fades
Will you still be here if I have nothing new to say
You are so accomplished, and I'm still finding my way

Maybe it's just my anxiety cuz we're so different,
baby, maybe it's just the red wine talking.
Cuz you're in a different country
I used to say, if you're going to fall in love with me, do it the right way.
Don't fall in love with my pretty face, it will age
Don't fall for my body, it will change
Fall in love with my soul, or don't fall in love with me at all

I know I'm crazy, but you're crazier for holding on
Sometimes I wonder if I'm doing anything wrong
Sometimes I see us turning a house into a home
Dancing in the kitchen

Arguing over how you like your food with a lot of black pepper and salt
And those moments we do nothing but in the silence feel like we belong
Sometimes I wonder if you feel the same way
Sometimes I wonder if you're meant to be the one who stays.
The one that changes my ways
The one who turns me into a wife
The one that I can spend the rest of my life with

Sometimes I wonder if this is too good to be true.

Sex, Weed, and Big City Dreams

My hands be on your hair.
My tongue be in your mouth.
And we be skipping town.
My body be wrapped around your sheets
Just like when I was 23
And we were high on sex, weed, and big city dreams

If it were up to me
We would have it so smooth, so easy
I would call you my baby for life
I would have the courage to stay
I would apologize for running away

If it were up to me
We would have taken graduation pictures holding our degrees
We would have bought the beach house of our dreams

If it were up to me
I would travel back in time
To that sex tape we made that July
When I was yours, and you were mine,
you're living rent-free on my mind

If it were up to me
I wouldn't be so scared to try
I would tell you how I feel
I wouldn't be so afraid and shy
I wouldn't waste so many years
I wouldn't say goodbye

My Ghost Friend

My ghost friend
comes back to visit me in my dreams
Maybe he's only a product of my fantasies
He left, but somehow his energy stayed
He sits beside my bed at night,
and I tell him about my life just to break the routine

My ghost friend,
I tell him I've fallen in love again
What an irony of life—when I loved him then,
he didn't love me, only saw me as a friend

My ghost friend,
a healer's soul who could set my heart on fire
My ghost friend,
you were right when you first met me
my heart was completely shattered
My ghost friend, what became of your life?
Under the full moon I remember you in every song

Your voice stayed recorded in my room
Sometimes it feels like you're listening along
So many years have passed since you left my life
I only hope you found your happiness,
even if it wasn't a life shared with mine

My ghost friend, I finally let you go
Maybe your memory follows me because it's April
And the question still stays with me,
because I never saw you again

Mi Amigo Fantasma

Mi amigo fantasma
En mis sueños me ha vuelto a visitar
Puede ser producto de mis fantasías
Él se fue y se quedó su energía
Él se sienta al lado de mi cama
Y le cuento de mi vida para matar la rutina

Mi amigo fantasma
Le cuento que me he vuelto a enamorar
Qué ironía de la vida cuando yo lo amaba
Él no me quería solo me vea como una buena amiga

Mi amigo fantasma
Alma de curandero de encenderme como fuego
Mi amigo fantasma
Tenía razón cuando usted me conoció
Tenia hecho mierda el corazon
Mi amigo fantasma qué será de su vida
Bajo la luna llena lo recuerdo en cada canción
Su voz se quedó registrada en mi habitación
A veces me parece que me escucha también

Han pasado tantos años desde su partida
Solo espero que haya logrado la felicidad
Aunque no fue compartir su vida con la mía

Mi amigo fantasma lo dejé ir
Será que su recuerdo me persigue porque es abril
Y la duda se me queda clavada
Porque nunca más lo vi

Better

Trying to put the pieces together
But I'm not 23 anymore, and I left
So you could find better
I thought you deserved better

And I'm so proud of you and all you overcame
I see your light guiding me through the night
I hear your voice deep in the back of my mind
And I stare at the moon til midnight

I started ignoring your calls and messages
Cuz I couldn't be your friend
I couldn't sleep with you and then go back home
Feeling the anxiety and the emptiness
Knowing well, you would be moving on to the next
You were only getting better

I still remember the last night together
Driving home at 4 am
Knowing you were catching a flight again
You were getting better
And I could taste your lips on mine
Even if you were miles away
But I never thought you would stay
So please forgive me for realizing too late
I could be better

11:11

It was more than physical.
It was more than chemical.
It was more than an energetic bond
It was the words to a song only they know
It was the rhythm they both sought

He led, she followed.
He remembered who he was
She surrendered to the call.

It was something so powerful it couldn't be
explained
Time and space didn't matter
Although apart, they were always together
She felt him in the morning on her drives to work
He has left an imprint on her heart
She knew the moment she met him that she would
never forget him

He was from another life.
Her eyes saw in him her truth
That one that she was running from
In his reflection, she saw the unlearning that had to
be undone

Neither said I love you with words
But also neither said goodbye
They each had to find one another
To find the light within each other
That they both had forgotten

I'm scared to fall in love again,

the last time left me half-undead,
a hungry, restless zombie then,
adrift in lonely seas instead,
my shattered heart in shards of red.

A shot of tequila and anxiety,
what once was joy and sweet complicity.
I'd been an optimist since childhood days,
but life, through blows, changed all my ways.

Until the day that you appeared,
my whole philosophy was rearranged.
I lied and said it was just chemistry,
but we're two mad souls, beautifully strange.

At last I found the ship's true captain,
the one I dreamed of all my life.
You came along and painted sunsets
across the evenings of my days,
and with a thousand kisses
you stretched my nights in endless ways.

Your honey-colored eyes enchanted me;
one night we danced beneath full moonlight's spell,
and there I gave you soul and sanity,
my skin as well.

It was a fleeting summer love,
yet still you chose to stay.
You saw in me what once had failed,
and I saw in you what life had kept away.

Your madness, your way of being,
a poem by Mario Benedetti,
two glasses of wine, romantic music,
old songs played slow and steady.

Turn off the lights, just feel it start:
the pounding rhythm of the heart.
Ever since you came along,
Cupid struck his arrow strong.

Tengo miedo de volver a enamorarme

La última vez que lo hice me dejó moribunda como
zombie y sin hambre
Navegando en los mares de mi soledad
Con el corazón partido en mil pedazos

Un trago de tequila y ansiedad
Que un día era alegría, amor con amistad
Era optimista desde niña
Pero a golpes realista me volvió la vida

Hasta que llegaste tú
Y mi filosofía cambiastes
Me mentía y decía que era solo química
Pero vos y yo somos dos locos
Encontré al capitán del barco
Con el que soñé toda la vida

Llegaste tú y a mis tardes les pintaste atardeceres
Y con mil besos las noches alargaste
Y me hechizaron tus ojos color miel
Bailamos una noche bajo la luna llena
Y te entregué mi alma, mi cordura y mi piel

Era un amor fugaz de verano
Y te quedaste a mi lado
Viste en mí lo que en el pasado falló
Y en ti vi lo que siempre me faltó

Tu loccura tu forma de ser
El poema de Mario Benedetti
Dos copas de vino música romántica
A la Antigua a la Medida
Apaga la luz y siente cómo late el corazón
Desde que llegaste tú
Cupido me flècho

Five More Minutes

You don't know sorrow.
 till you taste your own tears,
 You don't feel fear
 till it lives in your fears.
You never know
 What a memory costs,
 until time keeps moving
 And you see what is lost.
Give me five more minutes —
 just one more day,
 one more bike ride
 on the schoolyard way.
One more Friday night,
 "Mom, how do I look?"
 One more Saturday sigh
 When you close your book.
Give me "take your sweater,
 The night will be cold,"
 five minutes hearing
 Your guitar softly told.
I'm not ready yet
 to let you go —
 The world keeps spinning,
 But mine moves slowly.
They say life's unfair,
 Some hearts hurt more,
 So I smile in public.
 like nothing is sore.
I walk, I pray,
 I try to be strong,
 But all that I want
 is to turn back time's song.
Give me "Did you take my lipstick?"
 "Can I borrow your shoes?"
 "That boy's no good,"
 and your gentle rules.
 "Did you eat today?
 Too much coffee again?"

Five minutes of you —
I'd trade anything.
I never knew
 These small things I'd miss
 would one day become
 My definition of bliss.
So promise you'll fight,
Please promise you'll stay.
 Stand by my side
 on graduation day.
 Help choose my dress,
 meet the kids I'll raise,
 hold all my tomorrows
 inside our yesterdays.
Just five more minutes,
 That's all I pray —
 And we'll paint together.
 when this sickness fades away.

No Trust in Us

Every time I try to let you in and trust you.
You let me down. You say you won't do it again,
and I get my hopes up, then I watch them fall each time...
And I know you're a master at your craft.

You don't have to lie cuz I can read it in your eyes
You don't have to pretend anymore
I see you're always going to be a revolving door

And here I thought I could finally trust in love
Here I thought you could be the one
But here I am left pretending I don't care
Here I am, left hugging the pillow tight
Pretending you're not there

Here, I thought I could trust
But you're always falling into the same traps
I think your love sounds more like lust
I know I could start over and move on
I've done it before, so it shouldn't take long
But I got used to having you around

Pretending you love me even if your actions prove you don't
I know you're not perfect, and neither am I
But if I can't trust you, this should end with goodbye

It's been three years, baby.
Three years of he will change, maybe
Three years of us it won't happen again
But my patience and my trust are at their wits' end
There's no trust in us

2020

Dreamer

Hopeless Romantic

Old Soul

ROOTS

Where healing begins beneath the surface.

Healing did not arrive as relief.

There was no morning where I woke up and felt whole again. Instead, there was quiet. There was space where constant thinking used to live. Without the noise of the relationship, I was left with myself, and I did not know who that person was yet.

I had spent so much time learning how to love someone else that I never learned how to understand myself. When the distraction disappeared, every emotion became louder. I noticed patterns I once ignored. I saw how often I accepted less than I needed. I recognized the ways I confused attention with affection and stability with security.

Growth was not beautiful at first. It was uncomfortable. It was sitting with memories I wanted to avoid. It was acknowledging that I had abandoned my own boundaries long before anyone crossed them. I had to unlearn the idea that love required sacrifice of self. I had to forgive the version of me who stayed because she believed she deserved no better.

There were days I wanted to go back simply because it was easier than becoming someone new. Starting over meant making decisions without seeking permission, trusting my instincts, and learning to be alone without feeling unwanted. I had to rebuild routines, friendships, and dreams without attaching them to another person's presence.

Nothing on the outside looked different yet, but everything inside was rearranging. My identity was no longer defined by who loved me. I began asking new questions: What makes me feel safe? What do I enjoy when no one is watching? What kind of life actually belongs to me?

This section exists in the unseen work — the slow rebuilding, the nights of reflection, the small choices that eventually changed me. Roots grow underground. No one celebrates them because no one sees them.

But they are the reason anything survives.

Pretend

From a young age, I learned to pretend
Pretend the house wasn't on fire
Pretend my life wasn't hanging from a telephone wire
Pretend the tears weren't rolling down my cheeks
Pretend I wasn't holding my breath underwater
Pretend I had it easy and everything was given to me

Pretend I live the soft life
While most days, I struggle to survive
But don't let them see your weakness
Don't show them you are different
Swallow your pride and stuff your empathy
We live in a world where there's no humanity

Pretend like your life is not in limbo every two years
Pretend like you're not paying into a system
that doesn't care about you
Red White, and blue
They are only half the truth

Pretend like your future is not unclear
Pretend as if you belong here
baby just pretend
Cuz you know all suffering comes to an end

Queen of Overthinking

I'm the queen of overthinking
Some nights, I wake up drenched in sweat with anxiety
But you couldn't tell cuz I learned to pretend
Hide my faults under a smile
She's as happy as can be
My disguise has always been playing the part
And I believe it for a while

I'm the queen of overthinking.
But you couldn't tell by how hard I push back
There's always coffee in my cup
There is always a new plan, something to do
So I don't have to sit with my own thoughts
In the dark, those demons love to talk

I'm the queen of overthinking, but hey
Don't I make it look easy, don't I make it look good
 Don't you think sometimes you are misunderstood
The American Dream seems dead
All my plans seem to change day by day
They sold us a dream that turned out to be a nightmare

I'm the queen of overthinking, but life ain't fair
I'm just here playing ball
Watching how the sky falls
Considering whether therapy would help at all

I'm the queen of overthinking.
Mastermind, good things take time.
Maybe it's this glass of wine that got me talking
Maybe some of us were born too wild to be tamed
Our old souls can't take the pain
Everyone is looking for someone to blame

In the end, we're all the same.

Reina de Sobrepensar

Soy la reina de sobrepensar.
Algunas noches despierto empapada en sudor por la ansiedad
Pero no podrías notarlo porque aprendí a fingir,
a esconder mis fallas detrás de una sonrisa
"Está tan feliz como puede estar", dicen de mí
Mi disfraz siempre fue interpretar el papel,
y por un rato incluso me lo llego a creer

Soy la reina de sobrepensar
Pero no podrías notarlo por lo fuerte que sé resistir
Siempre hay café en mi taza,
siempre hay un nuevo plan, algo que hacer,
para no tener que sentarme con mis propios pensamientos
En la oscuridad, a esos demonios les encanta hablar

Soy la reina de sobrepensar, pero oye,
¿no hago que parezca fácil?, ¿no hago que se vea bien?
¿No sientes a veces que tú también eres incomprendido?

El Sueño Americano parece muerto,
y mis planes cambian día tras día
Nos vendieron un sueño
que terminó siendo pesadilla

Soy la reina de sobrepensar, pero la vida no es justa
Solo estoy aquí jugando la partida,
mirando cómo el cielo se derrumba,
preguntándome si la terapia ayudaría en algo

Soy la reina de sobrepensar
Mente maestra: las cosas buenas toman tiempo
Quizá es esta copa de vino la que me hace hablar
Quizá algunos nacimos demasiado salvajes para ser domados
Nuestras almas viejas no soportan tanto dolor
Todos están buscando a alguien a quien culpar

Al final,
todos somos iguales.

Divine Love

I feel your energy all around me
Is this in my head? Am I going crazy
To believe will meet again in divine timing
A year ago, if someone mentioned 1111, I would be laughing,
never believed in that kinda thing.
Til you collided with me, the catalyst that brought my
awakening

Forced me to face reality
Now I'm waiting 1111 wishing on a star
I know you know who you are
For now, it's easy to love you from afar
We're like the sun and the moon
Forbidden love can't see each other in the dark, can't touch,
but damn, we light a spark.

It's gonna take another universe.
For the imprint you left in my heart
We're like the sun and the moon
Both rise but can't stay side by side
Your ego gets in the way, and I can't swallow my pride
We're like the sun and the moon
Will we find a way to make things right

I want your long night drives.
I want the flowers just because
I want you to hold my heart and guide me through the dark
I'll be your light in the tunnel
When you think you're unbalanced and fumble
I'll be your scale, I'll be your armor
I'll be your sun, you be my moon

Desaprender

Tienes que ser fría, tienes que ser hielo
no te apresures tanto a ceder por consuelo
nena, algunas cosas toman tiempo
ignora al corazón, escucha al pensamiento
sabes muy bien que estás viendo señales

No hagas tonterías, no actúes el papel
aléjate, aléjate y no mires hacia atrás
recoge los pedazos y confía en Dios

Todos quieren meterse en mi cabeza
los teléfonos están en "no molestar" esta noche
quiero dormir en mi propia cama
hay tanto que desaprender
pero baby, algunas cosas toman tiempo
no te apresures, tu corazón está en intervención
escucha a tu intuición

chica, sabes lo que vales
perdónate por haberte conformado con menos
no te quedes quieta, ponte tus mejores zapatos de baile
solo los que no vinieron a perder
Basta de tonterías, mírate al espejo, eres hermosa
solo tienes mucho que desaprender

aún no te has perdonado
como si hubieras congelado tu corazón en un estante
Ve al gimnasio y enfócate en ti
reprograma tu mente
desaprende el modo supervivencia
toda la mierda por la que pasaste queda atrás
y te amarás a ti misma hasta el final

Borré todas las apps de citas de mi teléfono
no me molesta despertar sola
dar ese primer sorbo de café
intentar beber más agua cada día
escribir en mi diario cada mañana o cada noche
quedarme en casa viendo películas con una botella de vino
porque sé que sanar toma tiempo
desaprendiendo lo que fui, para volver a ser yo.

When we dance the sorrow fades away,

on the floor our bodies burst in flame,
touch me softly, steal a kiss tonight,
show me I'm still your baby all the same.
You take control and make sweet love,
in your arms I lose control above.

I want to silence reason in my soul,
I want to hear my heart take full control,
and between tequila and rum tonight
you whisper softly: my love.

No quiero perderte, baby,
dime que esto no es fantasía.
Sé que ya hemos pasado este camino antes,
pero quiero más todavía,
quiero todo de ti encima de mí.

Take me gently by the hand,
stop watching everyone who walks by.
Before my patience runs out
remember I just want your love

Let the troubles fade away,
let's be honest, you and I
are we meant forever
or are we just a moment in time

Bailando las penas son menos

Prendemos la pista los cuerpos son fuego
Acariciame y robame un beso
Demuestra que sigo siendo tu baby

Tú dueña hacme el amor
Quiero en tus brazos perder el control
Quiero olvidarme de la razón
Quiero escuchar a mi corazón
Y entre tragos de tequila y rum
Que me digas mi amor

I don't want to lose you, baby
Tell me this ain't a fantasy
I know we've been down this road before
But I want more
I want all of you on top of me

Llévame de la mano
Deja de ver a quien pasa por delante
Antes que me harte date cuenta
Solo quiero amarte

Que los problemas sean menos
Seamos sinceros
Somos para siempre
O somos un momento

Questions at 4:44 am

Questions at 4:44 AM
Cuz I'm up again
Toss and turn in bed
Can't sleep thinking, woke up dreaming
Can't remember the last time I was living

Questions at 4:44 AM
Who am I, who am I?
Who have I become, and am I really happy?
Or just numbed
Is this really reality?

Or am I coming undone
Am I just fearing what's next to come

Questions at 4:44 AM
Can't escape the clock
I'm back to where I started again
Feeling the energetic rush
Knowing damn well it ends with a crash

Questions at 4:44 AM
Caffeinated queen can't sleep
So I started questioning everything
Here we go again

Locked Door

There's a closet with a lock since 2019
All of my memories are buried in a box
Old clothes that belong to a younger me
One that I killed to put her out of her misery
The one who had innocent dreams
The one who was disappointed over time
Is facing reality

There's a closet screaming
To pack everything up and toss it in the trash
That I should have done it before
But I refused to look back
Now I'm looking within the walls
There's an old T-shirt from a rock concert
I was so drunk and high
At the moment, it felt like I was at the highlight of my life
There's an old pair of shoes I used to wear in high school
 cuz back then, I thought wedges were cool

An old picture frame
That girl, I don't recognize her
There's a closet being remodeled now
New bookshelves are being installed
And a new clothing rack
Shiny door with a new doorknob
It finally feels like it belongs in this house

Younger Me

And if younger me could see me now
I think she would be proud
I would start by telling her the path was not linear,
but it was raw, authentic, and real.

There were times it felt like it was all falling apart
Doors were closed without advance notice

She will wake up one day at 25 and feel unsatisfied
With her life, her career, and her relationships
And if younger me could see me now
She wouldn't believe how far we have come
In her late twenties, she would change course
Go back to school and earn a degree
Internships would lead to full-time positions
Doors she never thought she would walk through would open,
inviting her in

If younger me could see me now
I think she would understand
How nothing went as planned
But it was written in the stars
To fail and start over to rise above
To create a life she loves and feels good inside

Seasons

Some of my friends said friends til the end
But the moment I started chasing my dreams
They left
The moment I stopped chasing tequila
traded my wild nights for study halls
They couldn't understand
I had changed

They call it seasons.
And even the leaves start to dance in the wind for fall
I must confess, they helped me stay alive
And got stories I can't outlive even if I tried
I was hurt, I was healing, and dancing on table tops for fun
So they thought

Life of the party drinking Bacardi
They call it seasons for a reason
My track as a heartbreaker
Sure, I made a name for myself

Friend remained friends as long as I kept my heart on the shelf
I lacked boundaries and put everyone else's needs above my own
God forbid I changed at all
I started listening to my inner call
'Tis the season for leaving

Oligarchy

I'm lying if I didn't say
I've been having two meltdowns a day
I'm one foot in and out the door
Wondering if there's more to life

Sometimes I think about packing my bags
and starting somewhere new
If I can find another place and call it home
If I can start over across the ocean
Wait til I get my degree, it wasn't handed to me

I could move to Rome or Spain
Somewhere where I can numb this pain
Cuz it looks like this was never my country
I falsely pretended I could live the American dream
But it's an oligarchy

American Dream

I have been working my butt off all summer long
Just for you to say you don't see how far I've come along
I've been walking this path all alone

You don't see the mission, I am guided by my intuition
You're quick to critique, but don't make decisions
You're easy to fall short when it doesn't come easily

Don't bother to see the work behind the scenes
You just want to see that fruition

I'm making a name for myself.
I'm leaving my legacy behind.
In a couple of years, all the hard work will pay off
All those long nights and drives
All those early mornings just to survive
It won't feel like I'm just getting by

It will be paid in full.
That will be my truth.

Deposit on the beach house of my dreams
Riding my sweet ride down PCH with the speakers blasting, red Corvette
Say, that's the American dream, honey
My kids will never know what a life with struggle is like.
They will have the financial freedom to do what they like.

Living the dream, baby
El sueño no termina
Living the dream, baby

Uncomfortable days are over, maybe.
Cuz doing what others won't to get better
The struggle is real right now, but it won't be forever
American Dream since she was sixteen

Innerchild

Child, I've always been too much.
Too much emotion, too much fire
Too much soul out of control
You could light a match
And burn the whole place down
And somehow still come out on top

Child, there's nothing to be afraid of
You're learning to believe in yourself
Leave second-act imposter syndrome out
You know who you are and what you're about
Child, the years have tried to harden you
The trials have done a number on you

But you're still standing tall.
You're still getting up each day and risking it all.

Child, I'm proud of you.
You wouldn't recognize yourself these days.
There's nothing left of silent melancholy.
You're no longer fitting the mold.
You're not acting small.
You learned to use your voice.
To filter out the noise

Niña interior

Niña, siempre he sido demasiado
Demasiada emoción, demasiado fuego,
Demasiada alma sin control
Podrías encender un fósforo
y prenderle fuego a todo el lugar,
y aun así salir por encima de todo

Niña, no hay nada que temer
Estás aprendiendo a creer en ti misma
No permitas que el síndrome
del impostor arruine este nuevo capítulo
Sabes quién eres y de qué estás hecha

Niña, los años han intentado endurecerte,
las pruebas han dejado su marca en ti
Pero sigues de pie, erguida.
Cada día te levantas y lo arriesgas todo.

Niña, estoy orgullosa de ti.
Hoy en día no te reconocerías.
Ya no queda nada de aquella melancolía silenciosa.
Ya no estás tratando de encajar en el molde.
Ya no te haces pequeña.
Aprendiste a usar tu voz.
A filtrar el ruido

Later

Later, the coffee turns cold
Later, the chances you had won't hold
Later, the sun moves on
Later, there's nothing left of the things we left for later on

Later, life rearranges
Later, a new routine remains
We realize too late
What was truly important

Later, the clock won't stop
And time will never return

Later, all that's left is the urge to cry
To run through the streets and scream to the sky
Because I didn't see it before
Because I chased money, a title,
the dream of being someone important
And today it's worth nothing at all

Despues

Después el café se enfría
Después las oportunidades se van
Después el sol se irá
Después no existe lo que dejamos para después

Después la vida cambia
Después hay una nueva rutina
Después nos damos cuenta tarde
De lo que era de verdad importante
Después el reloj no se parará
Y el tiempo no regresará

Después solo quedan las ganas de llorar
De querer salir a la calle a gritar
Porque no me di cuenta antes
Porque siempre perseguí el dinero, el título,
el sueño de ser alguien importante
Y hoy no vale nada

Let it Rain Teardrops

Niña caprichosa y complicada
She feels it all
So sensitive for this cruel world
No one sees the tears she cries
She wipes them clean the moment she is done with her shower

Niña didn't they tell you to guard your heart
You keep healing
You keep transforming your pain into art
Hide the way you feel
smile for the photographs
And don't forget to laugh it off
Just don't let them see a teardrop

So much injustice is being served.
Don't let it get to you; it's not your problem
Just observe, be quiet, and polite

Niña, why do you always have to hide
How do you feel inside

Let it out til it rains from your eyes
Let it pour from the deepest parts of your soul
Let it rain teardrops
Let it fall
Let it rain teardrops

Transmute your words into hope.
You're allowed to feel it all.

Train

They asked me today
If I were ready for the next chapter.
I smiled and said, clueless as can be.
A part of me has packed her bags;
A part of me is afraid of the unknown.

I know the goal, but I'm still paving the path.
and what if I'm misled,
What if I drift off course?

They asked me today
If I'm ready to let go and trust God.
I smiled and said, " It's the unlearning.
the surrender of the need to always be in control.

Change is scary,
And not holding the pen is terrifying.
I'm a writer; I like an outline,
a skeleton I can shape
and mold to my design.

They asked me today
The questions that keep me up at night:
Am I ready for what's next?
As I hold the ticket in my left hand,
all that's left to do
is stepping onto the train.

Hey Blondie

Hey blondie
It's been a good ride.
Too many nights we can't outlive
Too many shades to coverup the gray skies
My alter ego
We had fun, oh, we were always on the run

Hey blondie
We bleached our roots too many times
We gave different names at bars on Friday nights
We decorated our silhouette with new ink
And we laughed at our problems in the morning
light
Pretending the ship didn't sink

Hey blondie
You were good to me
You were my healing phase
Baby, the surviving golden age
The swipe right, swipe left
You help me cope with my ptsd
And giving back a diamond ring

But it's time to say goodbye.
And come back to my roots.

Hey blondie
It took some time
But we made it to the other side.

Hey Rubia

Hey, rubia,
qué buen viaje fue este.
Demasiadas noches que no se pueden desvivir,
demasiados colores para tapar los cielos grises
Mi alter ego...
la pasamos bien, siempre corriendo de un lado a otro

Hey, rubia,
nos decoloramos las raíces demasiadas veces
Dábamos nombres distintos en los bares
los viernes de noche
Le fuimos sumando tinta nueva al cuerpo
y nos reíamos de los problemas con la luz de la mañana,
como si el barco no se estuviera hundiendo

Hey, rubia,
fuiste buena conmigo
Fuiste mi etapa de curarme,
mi edad dorada de sobreviviente
El swipe a la derecha, el swipe a la izquierda...
me ayudaste a sobrellevar el TEPT
y a devolver un anillo de diamantes

Pero es hora de despedirnos
y volver a mis raíces.

Hey, rubia,
nos llevó su tiempo,
pero llegamos al otro lado.

Garden

I'm gonna tend to my garden.
I'm gonna focus on me.
I'm gonna look within to find the answers I seek
All that I need is inside of me

I just have to believe.
Quiet the voices that try to confuse me
I'm gonna tend to my garden
I'm gonna start with the roots
And watch the seed fertilize
Make my dreams bigger than I realize
Live my life by design

I'm gonna channel all of my energy
I'll be the alchemist of my own destiny
I'm calling my power back to me
I'm gonna tend to my garden
Til the roses bloom and the leaves grow
And this garden is beautiful
It's where I belong

Jardín

Voy a cuidar mi jardín
Voy a enfocarme en mí
Voy a mirar hacia adentro para encontrar lo que busco en mí
Todo lo que necesito vive dentro de mí

Solo tengo que creer en mí
Callar las voces que intentan confundirme a mí
Voy a cuidar mi jardín
Voy a empezar por las raíces
Y ver cómo la semilla empieza a florecer

Hacer mis sueños más grandes de lo que puedo ver
Vivir mi vida como quiero ser
Voy a canalizar toda mi energía
Seré la alquimista de mi propio destino y mi guía
Estoy llamando mi poder de regreso a mí

Voy a cuidar mi jardín
Hasta que las rosas florezcan y crezcan las hojas así
Y este jardín sea hermoso para mí
Es donde pertenezco yo, aquí

Gitana

Enchanting gitana
Dancing through the night
Bare feet on the sand
A treacherous summer of tears she can't withstand
Since she was a child she speaks with the Full Moon's hand

The stars are her guides
Everything comes, everything goes
The world never stops turning as it flows
In winter even the coldest heart may change like snow

Gitana because she gives her soul
She reinvents herself each time life strikes a low blow
It shakes her balance for a while, soft and slow
And then she rises, shining bright in golden glow
As if she had never known a trace of sorrow

I'm a gitana, you'll never get used to me
I'm like the wind, give me wings and I'll fly free
I'm a gitana, I always say what I feel and what I see
I never stay in the same place too long to be me

Gitana: Spanish Gypsy, guided by intuition and free spirit.
It is used culturally or poetically to describe a woman with a
free spirit, nomadic by nature, or deeply connected to her
roots, music, and tradition.

Gitana

Gitana hechizera
Bailando en la noche
Pies descalzos en la arena
Verano traicionario de lágrimas y sueños
Desde niña habla con la Luna Llena

Sus guías las estrellas
Todo viene todo va
El mundo no para de girar
En el invierno todo cambiará

Gitana porque entrega su alma
Se reinventa cada vez que la vida le da un golpe bajo
La desestabiliza por un rato
Y luego brilla como el sol
Como si no supiera nada del dolor

Soy gitana, no te acostumbras a mí
Yo soy como el viento me dan alas y vuelo
Soy gitana siempre digo lo que siento
No me quedo en el mismo lugar por mucho tiempo

Ocean

What does the ocean mean to me
It means peace and serenity
Its depths bring me clarity in times of uncertainty

It commands respect
It's vast, powerful, and infinite
It can drown you or cleanse you

It guides you, the ocean holds memory
It speaks right through your soul
If you lie there quietly, you can listen to the melody
It always seems to bring me back to balance and harmony
It always brings me back to me

85

Océano

¿Qué significa el océano para mí?
Significa paz y serenidad para mí.
Sus profundidades me dan claridad
en la incertidumbre que hay aquí
Impone respeto.

Es vasto, poderoso e infinito.
Puede hundirte... o también purificar tu espíritu.

Te guía; el océano guarda memoria.
Habla directo a tu alma y a tu historia.
Si te quedas en silencio puedes oír su melodía.
Siempre me devuelve al centro y a la armonía.
Siempre me regresa otra vez a mí.

Belong

They say you belong
But this place doesn't feel like home anymore
So much hate is spread around
Be quiet, don't make a sound
They say you belong
But most days, I'm just surviving on my own

And nobody knows
The thoughts that cross my mind at 2 am

I'll always be seventeen, in ripped jeans, and a t-shirt
Even if I dress up now in a tailored blazer and slacks
Worked my ass off, but it's not good enough

They say you belong
But they don't tell you where
I'm climbing up the corporate ladder
Collecting degrees but drowning in debt
I'm putting all the pieces of the puzzle together
But they don't fit, they don't belong
And I find myself questioning every move I make lately

Wish I had a crystal ball or someone could look into my future
and tell me what the stakes are.
'Cause my patience is about to break
They say you belong
They say you belong
But you don't feel like you belong at all

hop Lovera Brand 2023

Sunsets

Graphic Designer

Fashion Modeling

BLOOM

Where there's confidence in rebuilding time after time.

I used to think healing meant becoming the person I was before everything happened.

Instead, I became someone I had never met.

The pain did not disappear, but it softened into understanding. I stopped searching for closure in other people and found it in acceptance. I no longer needed apologies I would never receive. I no longer needed to be chosen to feel worthy. I began to trust that the right things in my life would not require me to abandon myself to keep them.

For the first time, I was not loving out of fear of losing. I was living without constantly preparing for hurt. I learned that peace feels unfamiliar when you have lived in emotional chaos for too long. It is quiet. It does not beg for attention. It does not leave you guessing.

I started creating a life that did not revolve around survival. I laughed without guilt. I made plans without imagining who might leave. I allowed myself to feel joy without waiting for it to be taken away. I was no longer trying to return to the past. I was learning to exist in the present.

Loving myself did not look like perfection. It looked like boundaries. It looked like rest. It looked like forgiving my younger self for what she tolerated when she did not yet know her worth.

This section is not about forgetting what hurt me. It is about carrying the lessons without carrying the weight. I did not become unbreakable.

I became someone who knows she will rebuild, every time.

This is where I finally understand: starting over was never losing my life.

It was meeting it.

Resilient

Resilient not by choice
but
because my past made me
You're resilient he said
I heard it for the first time at 23 from a friend
You're resilient. What does it mean
He told me it means no matter what, you keep getting back up

Resilient not by choice, I thought.
Resilient
Yeah, the older I get, I guess that's a good way to describe me
Resilient, but nobody sees

The depths of the ocean
Powerful enough to drown me
When I only came to walk on the shore

Resilient if you are going through a hard time
You are just like me
You are guided by the moon and the sun
You are a star seed
a visitor in this galaxy
Resilient, we will always be

Old Guitar

I have an old guitar,
and a notebook full of songs
I used to sing my secrets and my deepest fears
to the mirror

I have an old guitar
that belonged to a sixteen-year-old girl
full of dreams
From a woman at twenty-three
who left everything behind
and started over

I have an old guitar
whose strings in my hands
feel unfamiliar and forgotten.

But I begin to tune them,
today I start to play them again
I have an old guitar
That calls out to me because I stopped doing
the things I once loved

Guitara Vieja

Tengo una guitarra vieja
Con un cuaderno de canciones
Antes le cantaba mis secretos y mis más
Profundos miedos al espejo

Tengo una guitarra vieja
De una chica de 16
Llena de sueños
De una mujer a los 23 que dejó todo atrás
Y empezó de nuevo

Tengo una guitarra vieja
Que en mis manos las cuerdas se sienten
Desconocidas y olvidadas

Pero empiezo a finarlas
Hoy empiezo a tocarlas
Tengo una guitarra vieja

Que me reclama porque dejé de hacer
Las cosas que me gustaban

Coffee with my younger self

If I had coffee with my younger self
She probably would show up 15 mins late
Blame it on traffic when she took too long to get ready,
listening to Green Day.
If I had coffee with my younger self
I would tell her that life gets better
It doesn't get easier,
but we learn to make the best of the hand of cards we've been given.

I would tell her some people are not meant to stay
They have a purpose and a season
If I had coffee with my younger self
I would tell her to stop hurting and hating herself
To stop people pleasing
And to learn to love her body as it changes

If I had coffee with my younger self
I would tell her to forgive herself for the things she couldn't change
Life gets better after 23, and you learn to cope with anxiety
If I had coffee with my younger self
I would tell her not to work off the clock
To put herself first is not selfish
To keep her standards high
Nonnegotiable boundaries

If I had coffee with my younger self
I would tell her it's ok to reinvent yourself
I would tell her to let go of control
To always give her heart and her soul
The pieces always fall together

Café con mi yo más joven

Si tomara café con mi yo más joven
seguro llegaría quince minutos tarde,
le echaría la culpa al tráfico cuando en realidad tardó demasiado en arreglarse
escuchando Green Day.

Si tomara café con mi yo más joven le diría que la vida mejora.
No se vuelve más fácil,
pero aprendemos a jugar mejor
las cartas que nos tocaron.

Le diría que algunas personas no están destinadas a quedarse.
Tienen un propósito y también una temporada.

Si tomara café con mi yo más joven le diría que deje de lastimarse
y de odiarse tanto,
que deje de querer complacer a todos
y aprenda a amar su cuerpo mientras cambia con el tiempo.

Si tomara café con mi yo más joven
le diría que se perdone por las cosas que no pudo cambiar.
La vida mejora después de los veintitrés y aprendes a convivir con la ansiedad.

Si tomara café con mi yo más joven
le diría que no trabaje fuera de horario,
que ponerse primero no es egoísmo.
Que mantenga sus estándares altos,
límites claros y no negociables.

Si tomara café con mi yo más joven
le diría que está bien reinventarse,
que suelte el control,
que siempre entregue el corazón,
y el alma entera.

Porque al final las piezas
siempre terminan encajando.

Place to Call My Own

I used to dance on tabletops for fun
My soul was wild, my heart on the run
I didn't trust easily
And I was good at playing the fools
who thought they were playing me
I was good at staying quiet
And leaving like a savage

Now all I crave is peace and serenity
A nice fireplace and listening to Spanish rock
A book on my lap and baking cookies
Drinking wine, reminiscing on my old life
Oh, those were some good times

But I want a safe haven.
No emotional roller coasters
I don't want any more trials
Find another soldier

Now I just want a steady hand to hold
A place to call my own
A lover who accepts me for who I am
And doesn't try to build me up as his fantasy
I just want to be me
Have a place to call my own

Dancing in the kitchen
Singing in the shower
My front patio overlooking the harbor
So I can watch the sunset to sunrise

After the darkness comes the light
A place to call my own, a place I call home

I fall in and out of depression every day
I'm just going through the motions, they say
I lost my spark and the glimmer in my eyes
Guess I'm not that great at wearing a disguise

But I always come back after each fall
I know how to stand up tall
Can't sleep much with this crippling anxiety
Don't really have time to dissect the complexity
So I'm leaving it all on the table
I'll pick it up when I'm able

Un lugar que sea mío

Solía bailar sobre mesas por diversión,
alma salvaje, corazón en rebelión.
No confiaba en nadie con facilidad,
y era experta en jugar
con los tontos que pensaban dominar.

Sabía quedarme callada sin explicación
y marcharme sin mirar atrás, sin compasión.
Ahora todo lo que anhelo es serenidad,
paz tranquila, simple claridad:

una chimenea, música suave al sonar,
rock en español y un libro al descansar.
Hornear galletas, vino para brindar,
recordando la vida que solía llevar.
Oh, sí... fueron tiempos de verdad.

Pero ahora quiero un refugio de verdad,
sin montañas rusas de intensidad.
No quiero más pruebas ni batallas que librar,
me cansé de luchar—
busca a otro soldado para pelear.

Ahora solo quiero una mano que sostener,
un lugar que sea mío al amanecer.
Un amor que me acepte tal cual soy yo,
que no intente moldearme en su ilusión.
Solo quiero ser yo, sin disfraz ni frío,
y tener por fin un lugar que sea mío.

Bailar en la cocina sin pensar,
cantar en la ducha sin parar.
Un patio mirando al puerto y al río,
para ver el atardecer volverse rocío,
y mirar la noche ceder al sol tardío.
Después de la oscuridad llega la luz,

un lugar que sea mío...

n lugar que sea hogar y cruz.
Caigo y salgo de la depresión cada día,
dicen que solo sigo la rutina vacía.
Perdí la chispa, el brillo en la mirada,
quizás nunca fui buena
llevando máscara prestada.

Pero siempre regreso después de caer,
sé muy bien cómo volver a crecer.
No duermo mucho con esta ansiedad feroz,
ni tengo tiempo de entenderlo todo en voz.

Así que dejo todo expuesto, sin vacío,
sobre la mesa... lo dejo ahí,
y volveré por ello
cuando vuelva a ser mío.

The Cool Air in December

The cool air in December
Always seems to bring me to my knees
The silence that lives inside of me

The clock is ticking louder.
And I start to analyze
All of the roads I travelled
All of the dreams I lived inside my mind

I'm taking inventory.
Another year that's come and gone
And I'm further than I was
But not quite where I want to be

They say life is a journey and not a race
But somehow I still feel like I'm behind
I see it when I look in the mirror
Time doesn't wait for anyone

And the thirties are slowly creeping up.
Some say it's the best years.
To have no fears

But questions like, will I ever find the right guy
to settle down with and take his last name
And I want to be a mom one day
But not anytime soon
Is that ok

The cool air in December

El aire frío de diciembre

El aire frío de diciembre
siempre logra ponerme de rodillas,
despierta el silencio profundo que habita dentro de mí.

El reloj suena más fuerte,
y empiezo a analizar
todos los caminos que he tomado,
todos los sueños guardados
que vivían en mi mente.

Estoy haciendo inventario:
otro año que llegó y se fue.
Estoy más lejos que antes,
pero aún no estoy
donde soñé.

Dicen que la vida es un viaje
y no una carrera veloz,
pero aun así siento a veces
que me he quedado atrás yo.

Lo veo cuando miro al espejo,
el tiempo no espera a la gente,
sigue su curso sin pausa
avanzando siempre al frente.

Y los treinta vienen llegando
cada día más presentes.
Dicen que son los mejores años,
los años valientes.

Pero llegan las preguntas:
¿encontraré al hombre ideal,
con quien construir mi vida
y su apellido llevar?
Quiero ser madre algún día,
pero no ahora, no todavía

Y me pregunto en silencio:
¿está bien
quererlo así también?

El aire frío de diciembre.

Looking Back, I Always Ran

Looking back, I always ran.
Guess it's not hard to understand
All the hurt, all the pain
Had me turn my emotions off
Anytime anyone got too close
I was saddling the horse

I know it's wrong
And I have no right
to come in and interrupt your life
But baby, what if I just realized
Looking back, I always ran
You never really stood a chance

I can see my player ways.
I led you on, but kept you at arm's length
I'm sorry, I was lacking strength
I was so afraid to fall
And break again

Looking back, I always ran.
Looking back, you had my heart.
I was too numb to see it
Looking back, it would have been us
I can't believe it

En Retrospectiva, Siempre Huía

En retrospectiva, siempre huía
Supongo que no es difícil de entender
Todo el dolor, todas las heridas
me hicieron apagar lo que sentía
Cada vez que alguien se acercaba de más,
yo ya estaba ensillando el caballo para escapar

Sé que está mal,
y no tengo derecho
a venir a interrumpir tu vida
Pero nene, ¿y si apenas lo acabo de entender?
En retrospectiva, siempre huía
Tú nunca tuviste oportunidad.

Ahora veo mis aires de Casanova
Te ilusioné, pero te mantuve a distancia
Lo siento, necesité perseverancia
Tenía demasiado miedo de enamorarme
y romperme otra vez

En retrospectiva, siempre huía
En retrospectiva, tú tenías mi corazón
Yo estaba demasiado dormida para verlo
En retrospectiva, habríamos sido nosotros
Y todavía no puedo creerlo.

RARE GEM

I'm a rare gem, a rock that hasn't yet been polished
No one knows me like I know myself
For a long time, I was left like an unopened book on a shelf
There were always shiny books with flashy names
Titles that were more captivating to the naked eye

I'm a rare gem, a rock that hasn't yet been polished
You see, my value lies in my beliefs
How I care for the people around me
My loved ones, friends, and family
You see, my value comes from within
It's my soul you should look out for
She knows how to be resilient
She is neither quiet nor obedient

I'm a rare gem, a rock that hasn't yet been polished
But you see, my value is not something you can find easily
Something you quickly overlook if you are looking for a model
that fits in size 2 denim jeans
Mine have holes in their knees
The color is not as vibrant as it used to be
My size nor my looks defines me
I'm not vain nor promiscuous
I'm simply me

GEMA RARA

Soy una gema rara, una roca que aún no ha sido pulida
Nadie me conoce como yo me conozco
Durante mucho tiempo me dejaron
como un libro sin abrir en un estante
Siempre había libros brillantes con nombres llamativos
Títulos que resultaban más cautivadores a simple vista

Soy una gema rara, una roca que aún no ha sido pulida
Verás, mi valor está en mis creencias
En cómo cuido a las personas que me rodean
Mis seres queridos, amigos y familia
Verás, mi valor viene de adentro
Es mi alma lo que deberías buscar
Ella sabe cómo ser resiliente
No es ni silenciosa ni obediente

Soy una gema rara, una roca que aún no ha sido pulida
Pero verás, mi valor no es algo que puedas encontrar fácilmente
Algo que pasas por alto rápido si estás buscando un modelo
que entre en unos jeans talla 2
Los míos tienen agujeros en las rodillas
El color ya no es tan vibrante como solía ser
Ni mi talla ni mi apariencia me definen
No soy vanidosa ni promiscua
Simplemente soy yo

The Sun Comes Out

If they ask me about life
I'd say I learned to fall without a parachute
But also to get back up and give it my all
I don't lose my mind anymore
Now I just trust in God and in destiny

Everything changes
The world never stops turning
Opportunities come and go
Today you're up and tomorrow you could be down

Enjoy the moment
Because in the end that's what makes us human

If they ask me about life
I learned to play the cards I was dealt
In everything, I give my heart
Otherwise it wouldn't be me

If they ask me about life
You just have to live it
Wake up early
Drink coffee and watch the sun come out
The sun always comes out

Sale el sol

Si me preguntan de la vida
Diría que aprendí a caer sin paracaídas
Pero también a levantarme y darle con todo
Ya no me desespero
Ahora solo confío en Dios y en el destino

Todo cambia
El mundo no para de girar
Las oportunidades viene y van
Hoy estás arriba y mañana puedes estar abajo
Disfruta el momento
Que al final es lo que nos hace humanos

Si me preguntan de la vida
Aprendí a jugar con las cartas que me tocó
En todo entrego el corazón
Si no, no soy yo

Si me preguntan de la vida
Hay que solo vivirla
Despertarse temprano
Tomar café y ver cómo sale el sol
Siempre sale el sol

A Quiet Life

I want a quiet life,
so that when people ask me about it
there isn't much to tell
Today, all I want is peace of mind

Romances like bonfires,
not the kind that poison and destroy
Health for my family,
moments with my friends
because the years are slipping by.

I want a quiet life.
Those days are over,
alone in my room,
crying with loneliness.

I want a quiet life,
I want a quiet life
to wander the world,
to live new experiences,
not to miss a single second.

I want a quiet life
What a life I live
in my fantasies.

Vida Tranquila

Quiero una vida tranquila
Que cuando me pregunten
No haya mucho que contar
Hoy solo quiero paz mental

Romances como fogataas
No de los que envenenan y matan
Salud para mi familia
Momentos con mis amigos
Que los años se nos van

Quiero una vida tranquila
Ya se acabaron esos días en el cuarto
Llorando Soledad
Quiero una vida tranquila
Quiero una vida tranquila
Ir recoriendo el mundo
Vivir nuevas experiencias
No perderme ni un segundo
Quiero una vida tranquila
Qué vida la mía
En Mis fantasias

Don't

I've been lied to, I've been broken, I've been soft and outspoken
I've been played, I've been crushed, and opened wounds don't heal fast
It has taken years to fight back tears and pick myself up

So if you're gonna love me
Don't fall in love with my pretty face (it will age)
Don't fall for my body (it will change), fall in love with my soul
Or don't fall in love with me at all
Cuz I don't need another somebody
Who turns into nobody
When I'm seeking my one and only

I unpacked all my baggage.
I got my self-worth back, my mind is in check
My heart is open to receiving
I'm letting divine timing bring you to me
But you'd better understand I come with a past and boundaries
you must respect. If you're trying to be my man

I learned the hard way that not everything that shines is gold
Not everyone who smiles is pure
So you'd better take your time
I'll be listening to the universe and asking God for signs

I'm not expecting you to be perfect.
Be weird, be loud, be crazy,
and be just my favorite type of lazy Sunday morning.
Coffee to go on my way to work
Quote of the day to start my day right
You'd better love to dance on Friday nights

I feel the sun on my skin

I fill my lungs with air
Listen to the ocean call, and I have no cares

Peaceful and serene
A view you can't picture in a magazine
I feel the summer heat

Walking down Pacific Coast Highway
I live my life my way
I hear the birds sing in the morning
I taste the first sip of coffee

Some of the nicest people I know are covered in ink

And some of the most judgmental don't dare skip church on Sunday
They smile in your face and then gossip
About your plans on Friday

Some of the nicest people I know
Went through something that made them grow
But they are judged for making a mistake
Like everyone is perfect
And can't have any flaws to be worth it

I'll tell it to you straight.
I smell fake a mile away.
Some of the nicest people I know
Always take the blame

**Algunas de las personas más buenas
que conozco están cubiertas de tinta,**

y algunas de las más juzgonas no se atreven a faltar
a la iglesia el domingo
Te sonríen en la cara y después andan chismeando
sobre tus planes del viernes

Algunas de las personas más buenas que conozco
pasaron por algo que las hizo crecer
pero las juzgan por haber cometido un error
como si todos fueran perfectos
y como si para valer algo hubiera que serlo

Te lo digo sin vueltas:
al falso lo huelo a kilómetros.
Algunas de las personas más buenas que conozco
son las que siempre terminan cargando con la culpa

Qué ironía de la vida

Siempre quise ser grande
Y hoy quiero volver a ser niña

A cantar por la calle
A bailar en el cuarto
A robarle un par a mamá de zapatos

Miedo

Tengo miedo que esto sea pasajero
Que la vida me juegue una mala pasada
Y se me deramen las cartas
Tengo miedo que aparezca la mujer de tu vida
Y a mí solo me veas como una niña

Tengo miedo que lo nuestro tenga fecha de cautiva
Y es que tus ojitos color miel combinan bien con tu piel rojo atardecer
Perdóname si soy impulsiva
Y a veces las heridas de mi pasado me dominan
Tengo miedo de que mi ansiedad
No la pueda controlar y sé que me ves llorar

Perdóname por no saber hablar

I Belong in Spring

The leaves fall in autumn.
Snakes shed their skin
People change, and sometimes a loss
It's a win

If you are stuck in a mental prison
You know the feeling well
It's the in between
The transformation is being felt
But only from within

Changing is scary
Your thoughts are making you guilty
Like evolving is considered a sin

I always hated winter.
I belong in spring

I'm Whole On My Own

It's Sunday afternoon
I am walking on water
I have an iced cold brew in my left hand
The wind is gently blowing on my hair

I stop, and I am there.
It's not a destination.
I am not chasing anything
It's a feeling of serenity

I'm whole on my own

In Another Life

In another life
I suppose we got it right
I was able to mold to your perfection
I conformed to the traditions and your religion

In another life
We were happy
I didn't have to shrink or dim my light
And we got the beach house, the backyard, and the kids
Like we dreamed

In another life
It was you and me
We were as beautiful as poetry
We danced in perfect synchronicity

In this life, I couldn't live up to your fantasy
Without abandoning me
I am resurrecting
A beautiful mosaic art piece

Algo Que Te Haga Feliz

IMe dijeron: "Escribe algo que te haga feliz",
y me quedé pensando,
con lágrimas formando.

Tal vez el mar,
o las estrellas,
bailar bajo la luna llena,
cualquier cosa que me ayude a olvidar
esta pena.

Este frío que me cala los huesos,
este vacío que no lleno con nada,
este miedo que no me deja vivir.

Tal vez perderme por unos días,
cumplir con alguna fantasía,
algo que me devuelva la sonrisa.
Algo que me lleve de vuelta a mí.

Si eso me haría poder
escribir de algo que me haga feliz.

Rebirth

I looked into the mirror's face
and barely knew the soul in place.
Not even the shadow I used to be,
somewhere along the way I abandoned me.

I lost my plans, the dreams I knew,
the life I once believed was true.

I gave myself away instead
to save a love that now lies dead.
I dimmed my light little by little,
my heart grew cracks down to the middle,
for loving wildly, loving blind,
a reckless fire that burned my mind.

But now I rise much stronger than before,
no battle now I cannot endure.
Today the flowers bloom once more,
and my soul begins to be reborn.

Today I sing for life still mine,
for this wounded heart that still survives
battered, broken through the years,
yet somehow beating past the tears.

To rise again without the fear,
to be the self I once held dear.
There's still some time, the road is clear.
Rebirth begins right here.

Renacer

Me miraba en el espejo
Y no reconocía mi reflejo.
Ya no era ni la sombra que un día fui.

Me olvidé de mis planes, mis sueños,
Me olvidé de mí.

Por estar salvando lo poco que quedaba
de un amor que hoy no es nada,
Me fui apagando poco a poco
y me crecieron grietas
Por amar a lo loco.

Pero hoy vuelvo más fuerte que ayer,
Hoy no hay batalla que no sepa superar.
Hoy vuelven las flores a florecer
Y mi alma empieza a renacer.

Hoy canto por la vida que me queda,
por un corazón herido, maltratado,
pero vivo.

Renacer sin miedo,
ser quien pude ser,
Aún estoy a tiempo.
Renacer.

"SHE BELIEVED SHE COULD, SO SHE DID."

— R. S. Grey,
Scoring Wilder

2026

Poetry Author

Dancing Queen

Self Love

Acknowledgments

This book would not have been possible without the support, encouragement, and love of many people along the way.

First, I thank God for the strength, clarity, and resilience to continue writing even when the journey felt uncertain. His plans are bigger than mine.

To my family and friends, thank you for believing in me, encouraging me, and reminding me of my purpose during moments of doubt. Your support has meant more than words can express.

To La Poeta Publications for believing in me and my writing and my mentors, and individuals who poured wisdom into my life, thank you for helping shape the woman and voice behind these pages.

Also, I want to recognize Pablo Contreras Sánchez for helping translate the poems into English and Spanish versions, and Curtis Robideau for the photography in each section.

Finally, to every woman who has ever questioned her worth, struggled to start over, or fought to find her voice, this book is for you. It's never too late to be who you want to be.

About the Author

Melina Lovera is a writer, poet, and storyteller whose work explores resilience, identity, healing, and the quiet strength that comes from rebuilding oneself after life's most difficult seasons. Through deeply personal reflections and emotionally raw poetry, she captures the journey from heartbreak and uncertainty to self-acceptance and renewal.

Rebirth is her second poetry collection, inspired by moments of loss, growth, and transformation that shaped her voice and perspective. Her writing blends English and Spanish influences, reflecting the cultural and emotional layers that define her story. Melina was born in South America, Uruguay, and raised in Orange County, California.

Melina believes poetry is more than words; it is a space where vulnerability becomes strength and where readers can find pieces of their own story between the lines.

MENTAL HEALTH RESOURCES (CALIFORNIA)

National Domestic Violence Hotline
📞 1-800-799-7233
💬 Text: START to 88788
🌐 Online chat available
→ Free, confidential, available 24/7 in multiple languages

LA County Domestic Violence Hotline (24/7)
📞 (800) 978-3600

California Youth Crisis Line
📞 1-800-843-5200

National Sexual Assault Hotline
RAINN)
📞 800-656-4673

24/7 Mental Health Support

988 Suicide & Crisis Lifeline
📞 Call or Text: 988
💬 Chat available online
→ Free, confidential, 24/7 support for emotional distress, anxiety, depression, or crisis ()
Crisis Text Line
💬 Text HOME to 741741

SAMHSA National Helpline
📞 1-800-662-4357

CalHOPE Warm Line
📞 (833) 317-4673

→ Free emotional support for stress, anxiety, and overwhelm ()

California Mental Health Resources
🌐 mentalhealth.ca.gov

→ Free statewide programs, youth support, and wellness tools ()

NAMI HelpLine
📞 1-800-950-6264
→ Guidance, education, and mental health resources ()

APOLOGY LETTER

Dear Younger Me,

I apologize for not being able to protect you from the things that destroyed you. I put you in places where your value and worth was overlooked. I abandon you slowly, I let your dreams die and let your light run out. I let you pour yourself into others until you ran dry. I kept you in a mental prison for so long. I made you feel guilty for actions that were beyond your control. I didn't allow you to ask for help when you needed it the most and I taught you how to fake that everything was fine by masking your emotions and not allowing you time to process, to heal to grow and evolve.

I will NEVER do that again! My inner child you deserved so much more than I gave you permission to experience. Yes, we made a ton of mistakes, but we paid them in full and most importantly we learned to trust ourselves.

Dear Future Self,

We are stronger because we were forged by our inner fire. We became resilient and we continue to grow. We learned to live in the present. We are persistent and flexible with our methods. We are open minded and not afraid of winds of change that may come our way. We learned to apologize and let go of weight that we carried that didn't belong to us. We clear chakras, we listen to our guides and God and the universe. We set firm boundaries and we don't put ourselves in places that compromise our beliefs or values. We finally understood we are whole on our own. We love the woman we are becoming and we know REBIRTH is a journey not a destination.

xoxo

Melina Lovera